This book r...
below to ...
issu...

Bump-starting the Hearse

CIRCULATING
COLLECTION

MPB

D0434561

By the same author

The Bear Looked Over the Mountain
Treble Poets I (with Stephen Miller and Elizabeth Maslen)

Bump-starting the Hearse

Kit Wright

Hutchinson
London Melbourne Sydney Auckland Johannesburg

EAST SUSSEX

V.	MAC	INV. No.	6035	
CLASS No.	8 21. 914			H
BOOK No.	212085	950		

COUNTY LIBRARY

Hutchinson & Co. (Publishers) Ltd
An imprint of the Hutchinson Publishing Group

17-21 Conway Street, London W1P 6JD

Hutchinson Group (Australia) Pty Ltd
30-32 Cremorne Street, Richmond South, Victoria 3121
PO Box 151, Broadway, New South Wales 2007

Hutchinson Group (NZ) Ltd
32-34 View Road, PO Box 40-086, Glenfield, Auckland 10

Hutchinson Group (SA) Pty Ltd
PO Box 337, Bergvlei 2012, South Africa

First published 1983
Reprinted 1984
© Kit Wright 1983

The paperback edition of this book is sold subject to the
condition that it shall not by way of trade or otherwise
be lent, resold, hired out or otherwise circulated without
the publisher's prior consent in any form of binding
or cover other than that in which it is published and
without a similar condition including this condition
being imposed on the subsequent purchaser.

Set in VIP Melior by
D. P. Media Limited, Hitchin, Hertfordshire

Printed and bound in Great Britain by
Anchor Brendon Ltd, Tiptree, Essex

British Library Cataloguing in Publication Data
Wright, Kit
  Bump-starting the hearse.
  I. Title
  821'.914   PR6073.R52
ISBN 0 09 153311 2 ✓

Contents

Acknowledgements

Some of these poems first appeared in the *Times Literary Supplement*, *Poetry Review*, *Bananas*, *Quarto*, *Zip*, *Smoke*. Others have been included in the Arts Council anthology *New Poems 4*. Some have been broadcast by the BBC (Schools Radio) and Granada TV ('Live From Two'). To the editors and producers concerned acknowledgement is due.

Black Box

The star is falling so it prove a stone.
Flight Zero, moon, is flashing us goodbye.

Because we could not bear to be alone
We talked our deaths down nightly from the sky.

In darkness, in the Dreamtime, we have flown
Over the mountain where our picked bones lie.

The Specialist

Imagine you dreamed
you were nothing, taken
by a crying stranger, once
loved by you,

to the special room
where sat the specialist
and his huge head,
so it seemed, grew

straight out of a desk
by a tall window,
a lectern in glasses
against mad blue

and the hopeless words
fell out and died,
then the glasses gave their
professional view:

'The problem here –
there are several names for it –
the problem – several
strains of it too –

the problem's our old friend
death. That's one name for it –
several others, as
I've said, would do.

(There's death and death
and death and death
and death and death,
to name but a few,

but I think it as well
to stick to one, then
we know just where
we are, don't you?)

Massive D. Oh, there's
heartbeat, breath.
But loss of feeling, now
that's the clue.

There's nothing there
and never will be, love
can't get out and it
can't get through.

Bite on this darkness,
swallow this shadow:
I fear that's all
I can do for you.'

Imagine you dreamed this
end-stopped dream
and woke in a boiling
sheet-sweat stew.

Imagine you dreamed this
stone-cold dream
and woke and the whole cold
thing were true.

The Divine Comedy

Laugh? They were sick.
They rolled on the floor, they

Didn't seem to see it,
The funny side.

Doubled up, curled up,
Fell about, they

Pissed themselves, all
Utterly helpless,

Roared and screamed
And rocked and cried: they

Just couldn't see it.
Laugh? They died.

Frankie and Johnny in 1955

Many of the men wore damned great flannel trousers
With double-breasted blazers. Double-breasted women
  wore blouses

With pleated skirts or shiny black haunch-hugging dresses
On the night and the morning of the twin
  unpleasantnesses –

His shooting, her hanging – while I myself wore shorts,
Snakebelt and aertex, suitable for summer sports,

When Albert Pierrepoint hanged Ruth Ellis high
In Holloway Prison and I was too young to cry –

She, to die. Poor Ruth, I say:
She whipped out a .38, blew her lover away.

Now, Ruth was the last woman hanged on British earth
And David Blakely was of moneyed birth –

Public school, army, obsessed with racing cars,
Which he talked about all the time in clubs and bars –

Was a total shit, some say, which I think untrue –
I think he was as much of a shit as me or you –

Some say he was charming and friendly – alas for charm –
The grave leaves never a trace – well, he did her harm,

But not as much harm as she did him that day
She whipped out a damned great gun and she blew him
  away.

Well, Ruth was the Little Club night-club manageress
And had been through, seen through, much distress

Long before the killing. She'd a war-time child
By a GI who ditched her, divorce suit filed

From a mad alcoholic dentist who smashed her about:
Then: semi-pro loving in clubs. No doubt

Of the matter at all, time worked her so
Little Ruth was as hard as nails and as soft as snow

And the hurt she felt, and the love, and the hate
She fired point-blank from a damned great .38.

Oh, the reason little Ruth was standing in the dock
Was she loved him in the morning and she loved him
    round the clock

But people were stealing him. Ruth said, 'Well,
Can't see my loving man here, I'll see him in hell' –

And she wanted to die, did die, which she needn't have
    done
But she said in court, with that Smith and Wesson gun

She'd a fancy to kill him – wed him with a big black
    trousseau?
Yes, she wanted to die. But *he* didn't wish to do so

And I count it a shame that by South End Green
She wasted her lover with a damned great hand-machine.

She'd a powder compact that played *La Vie En Rose*,
She was taking French lessons, she'd a special film-actress
    pose

For photos, she was slender, she'd a small white face like
    an ox-eyed
Daisy and hair of pure peroxide

(That probably hanged her – at the trial a smart
Juror noted down: 'She's a TYPICAL WEST END TART')

And Blakely was a handsome and a likeable youth –
Spoilt ponce, too, violent bastard to Ruth,

Some say. Who's to judge? Oh, the judge could judge that
    day
He slipped on his little black cap and he slid her away.

Not much to say. She loved him but she hadn't got him,
Waited by the pub and when he came out she shot him

With a mixed spray of bullets to his head, his lungs, his
    heart:
It was theatre, my lovely, performance art,

But you didn't want to do it, they didn't want to do it to you
And they snipped your pretty white throat pretty nearly in
    two

Because, entirely, it was 1955:
Oh, I wish you were here, I wish you were alive

And I wish above all things unmade, junked down the
    spout,
That damned great side-arm that took your loving man
    out.

Your lifetime later, I think how nothing is freed
By time from its shadow, opacity of need,

The instant when it happens, in situ, on spec –
How nothing but detail breaks anyone's heart or neck –

Of how, little Ruth, in the first year of rock-and-roll,
You could tip young David down into the hole

Or how they could hang you on a Holloway hanging tree,
Poor little Ruth Ellis, two months before ITV.

The Fools in the Ground

Many big brains have cracked themselves open inquiring
Into the wiring of time, slow fuse, short circuit,
And wondering what in hell or heaven can work it

So

The hitherto indiscernible
In the bat of an eye proves
Non-returnable,

That which was
Inconceivable:
Irretrievable.

Nothing more deep than that nothing will keep is the
    wonder
That sundered these heavy heads at the seams,
Their findings: dreams,

Their own ghosts
Dying
Away from them

In morning light
That, to spite them, wouldn't
Stay for them.

No,

It's our own little try-on.
Wired and struck, to stand in the rain as it rains
On the many big brains of the fools in the ground that we
    die on.

Hardly Believable Horace and Hattie in Hell

Horace and Hattie, in cacophonous concert,
  Lived to a dual and discordant tune,
They could and they did disagree about everything
  Under the sun, and also the moon,
And if one said, 'Nice morning', the other infallibly
  Pronounced it a horrible afternoon,
And if either one triumphed in a point at issue
  (And no point was not) then the victory balloon
Would be savagely pierced when the narrowest opening
  For vengeance was glimpsed. They did not commune:
They spoke to each other to accuse, to exclude,
  To ensnare and enrage, to impair and impugn.

Which makes it the stranger that they slept together
  Where even in the night like poisonous rain
Exchanged unpleasantries dripped in the darkness –
  Miss no chance where a particle of pain
Might yet be extracted was their changeless motto
  And no opportunity passed in vain –
So they sharpened themselves like knives on each other
  Where once more sweetly they had lain
When theirs was a house where love was living
  Whose ghost would not sleepwalk again,
Never a shadow, never a whisper,
  Not a whisker, not a grain.

So Hattie died, and she died with a rattle
  That threw the points in Horace's head
And his heart on its journey grated, slowed
  And turned like an engine in a turning-shed
And headed back down through the wailing tunnel
  Of the years, of the cold things done and said,

And he went by the land and he came by the water
   Of unshed tears on wounds unbled,
And he lay on his back in his clothes in the morning
   On that reconsecrated bed,
Floor of the ocean of a marriage, and cried
   Like the sea, 'My love, my love is dead!'

Hopkins in Liverpool

In the oak-and-ivory church of St Francis Xavier,
    Arches recessional,
The poet Hopkins tangled with human behaviour,
    At the confessional.

How can I stand in the church of St Francis Xavier,
    Musk-scented wood,
And think that his passion, his music, his genius, his
  Saviour,
    Did no good?

    Pity them, did you, Father
    Hopkins, in their pain,
    Their terror and their hunger,
    Herded, dying upon
    Each other in the stinking
    Courts below the bows
    Of the high traders making
    For Nova Scotia snows?

    Comfort them, did you, Father,
    As the dark sank in
    Starved faces by the river,
    Open to the rain?
    Prayed with them, did you, waited
    By them, dying, saved
    For a heaven that you doubted
    From hell, that you believed?

    Tuberculosis, Father,
    Cholera. All you knew
    Of healing, as a mother,
    You fed them on the slow,
    Slow tide of the Lord's mercy:
    To agony, his ease.
    The Lord has got his fancy.
    To you, please, Father, peace.

The Losing of Liverpool

1

One freezing blue evening I spied him bestriding
  The steps of the ice-green Nigeria Club,
His boots wide apart and his fists in his pockets
  As the wind on his cheekbones drummed
    rub-a-dub-dub.

Below on the pavement two huge blue-black women
  Stood clenched in the ice of the salt-river breeze.
One sang out, 'Dis pussy, him *stay* private property!'
  'Right *say!*' he shouted, and bent at the knees

As, heartily rocking, all three of them, mocking
  The wind and the weather, became a big bell,
Chiming, and purple, and hurtling through everything:
  Don't know the joke, but I wish those three well.

2

Around this world I've travelled far
  To home behind this door,
But a prostitute with a walking stick
  I never did see before.

What are you doing here, ladies,
  On Huskisson Street,
After so many a summer
  Taking the day's heat
    And the loveless comer –
  Can anyone want you, *anyone*,
    Any more?

  Gash and thatch,
  Stood on the street here,
  Yelling and selling
  Snatch.

Some aren't fussy:
Stood on the street here
Shouting and touting
Pussy.

Exceedingly sleazy geezers
  Crawl Huskisson Street
In executive wrecks but they can't
  In the name of Jesus
    Be customers, can they?
Ladies —
          your poor old feet!

Around this world I've travelled far
  And still it seems to me
A prostitute with a walking stick
  No one ought to be.

3
And some so thin, so young, such almost children,
  Twisted flowers by the broken wall,
Ruined secrets in the giant's garden,
  Bitter blossom spilling in the fall.

4
People could get a good view of the empty docks
If they stood on the tops of these empty

Tower blocks, which grin
From the hill at the tide going out and the tide
Coming in. And seem
Like terrible beggarwomen in a horrible dream
Upon whom everything aimed
Has recorded a hit:
Eyes gouged out, teeth kicked in, throats
Rammed with shit,

They contained much life, many lives,
But it was no good,
They are all dead trees, the disease
Flies merrily from wood to wood.
Is it an accident, no, they are patterned
To get rather worse before they get
Vastly worse and then they get
Flattened. If they stood

On the tops of these empty tower blocks,
People could get a good view of the empty docks . . .

5

    . . . where the river
        the colour of liver
           whacks

    at the weeds
        in the cracks
           of the wall

    and the tall
        wharves rotten
           forgotten

    recall

    fuck all . . .

6

        but hear it for Joseph Williamson,
Remember the useful endeavour of Joseph Williamson,
The mole of Mason Street,
Who constructed surprises beyond the aspiring of man
Beneath his feet,
Whose element was the Underworld, whose Plutonic
Shade is the sand-
Stone forest of deepdown disremembered darkness
Felled by his hand,
Or umber and ochre meadow reaped for the aid
Of supervised labour,
His underfed Irish: tread softly on Joseph's ghost,
Your downstairs neighbour,

Whose thought was sound
When inside out and upside down he fashioned
His burial mound.

Who wandered from Warrington in at the age of eleven
In 1781,
Was lord of his own strange, dripping and literal suburb
Before he was done,
Who, youngest apprentice of Thomas Moss Tate, Esquire,
Tobacco Importer,
Twenty years later had eaten the family business
And married its daughter
To come in exceptional wealth to an odd retirement,
His cellar floor,
Whereunder he started to dig up that darkness whereby
He spread some more,

For who can explain
The excavation of nothing whatever for neither
Light nor gain?

7
In wombs and catacombs below
The air: in brownish-purple tombs

Of sombre echo where no moon
Illumined him among the bare

Wet-whispered caverns, dreamed-out rooms:
The waif of Warrington, I do

Believe, looked for his mother there.

Wailing in Wandsworth

Lovers who would pet and fondle
All along the River Wandle,
Running down through Wandsworth Town
    Leafily, are gone.
Factory excreta tumble,
Gangs prowl, sniffing out a rumble,
    And the cops move on
Cottagers disposed to fumble
In their lowly dwelling, humble
    Public jakes or john.

Where the lovers used to ramble
Adult Aid chain owners amble,
Strolling down through Wandsworth Town,
    Counting up the cash.
By the bridge, his fourteenth tipple
Claims the drunk, who takes a triple
    Length-and-value slash,
And the alders wind would ripple,
Poplar, beech rain loved to stipple,
    Are not even ash.

Still and all, I shouldn't grumble,
I who sit alone and mumble,
Writing down in Wandsworth Town
    My troubled Double Dutch.
I would never cause to stumble
From its grave, but let it crumble,
    Ancient pain, as such.
By the waters of the Wandle
Where the lovers used to fondle,
Where I craft this rhubarb rondel,
    Life is better: much.

The Boys Bump-starting
the Hearse

The hearse has stalled in the lane overlooking the river
Where willows are plunging their heads in the bottle-green
   water
         And bills of green baize drakes kazoo.
         The hearse has stalled and what shall we do?

The old don comes on, a string bag his strongbox.
He knows what is known about Horace but carries no tool
   box.
         Small boys shout in the Cambridge sun.
         The hearse has stalled and what's to be done?

Lime flowers drift in the lane to the baskets of bicycles,
Sticker the wall with yellow and powdery particles.
         Monosyllabic, the driver's curse.
         Everything fires. Except the hearse

Whose gastric and gastric whinnies shoot neutered tom
   cats
In through the kitchen flaps of back gardens where tomtits
         Wizen away from the dangling crust.
         Who shall restart the returned-to-dust?

Shrill and sudden as birds the boys have planted
Their excellent little shoulders against the lamented
         Who bumps in second. A fart of exhaust.
         On goes the don and the holocaust.

'Hoffa's a Goddam Hubcap':
An Idyll

(Jimmy Hoffa of the Teamster's Union, his body said to
have been disposed of in a car-crusher)

An old dirt road. A closing country sky.

Moon-absent and moon-shiny,
Spun to a standstill by the homely Diner
Where root beer washes down his Master's pie,

Jimmy reflects the tiny
Pines of Carolina.

Carpe Diem

When I was a six-foot twelve-year-old,
  My Grandad said to me:
Child of my heart, I could be wrong,
  But as far as I can see,
The way things are going, my boy, you'll be growing
  To a height of twelve foot three:

  Be that as it may,

  It's overkill, overkill,
  The worst thing that could happen
  Will:
  The world shall roll the world away:
  Seize the day.

Now I heard that right and I got that straight,
  Each word my Grandad uttered,
And I tried to seize the day but the day
  Proved slippery and buttered:
With the noon's advance, I floored each chance,
  So I didn't shout but muttered:

  Be that as it may,

  It's overkill, overkill,
  The worst thing that could happen
  Will:
  The world shall roll the world away:
  Seize the day.

So the days shot on and I shot up
  A foot and a half a year.
Alas, the world was at my feet
  Throughout my mild career,
But locked in my head was a tune from the dead,
  My Grandad at my ear:
  Sighing:

Be that as it may,

It's overkill, overkill,
The worst thing that could happen
Will:
The world shall roll the world away:
Seize the day.

Now I through the matchless, catchless days,
  Some shiny and some shitty,
Keep right on dying with the rest,
  Of terminal self-pity,
Through life sustained by this half-brained,
  Half-pertinent ghost-ditty:

Be that as it may,

It's overkill, overkill,
The worst thing that could happen
Will:
The world shall roll the world away:
Catch it falling,
Seize the day.

Catch it falling,
Seize the day.

Dungoblin

Come down, come down, you long-serving ladies of
    pleasure,
To Hove, to Rottingdean,
Where sea, where privet hedge are green
And a Tory sky
Has the rebel geranium's measure:
To Southport or
Liskeard,

After so many years hard
At the coal face of the libido,
Mes poules pas de luxe, come down, come, *tirez-*
Vous doucement les rideaux
On peaceful evenings with pollarded poodles
(Forsaken the stand-up and cash-down canoodles),
Chihuahua and chocs and the box and the balm

Of Dungoblin.

Forgotten, the day job, the night job, the so-much-a-go job,
Abandoned, the blow job,
Come down,
O come away from Humping Town
And snooze where the little waves lick themselves like cats
Under the green head
And the old folks' flats

At Dungoblin.

Lila's Song

Spent my loving days unlearning
Love for a man with the trick of turning
Every little thing to his
Disadvantage:
That was the *only* trick
The creep could play:
Never loved me: pissed as a parrot
Every night and day:

Bundle it up, then, ladies.
Hump it down to the river, gotta tip it away.
Drown it dark and drown it deep.
It will kill you if it keep.

So wobble it off
To the knacker's yard of shagged-out marriages,
To the wrecker's place
Where the chained Alsatian
Howls all night through the gap in the gate –
Junk it, dump it, cash it for scrap –
Sling it – you got no
Time to wait –

So wheel it in
To the morgue of rigid love affairs,
To the charnel house
Where the perfect toys dry-rot in stacks: kiss
Each little stick, each
Stone goodbye: just
Let that
Hurt thing
Die: now

Bundle it up, you ladies.
Hump it down to the river, gotta tip it away.
Let it sink and let it sleep.

It will kill you if it keep.

Like a Fairy Tale

When Lynda came home from college her very first year
(Her very first try)
With the Senior Personal Freshness Challenge Bowl,
Father hugged and hugged and hugged her:
Mother just stood in the drive and cried,
She felt so
Proud inside.

There was quite a bit of chat where Father worked
At the National Westminster Bank.
'You know that Lynda Hodgkiss up Merrivale Rise –
Pocketed the Personal Freshness Prize!'
'What, Lynda Hodgkiss, I thought she stank!'
'That's Lynda Hargreaves.' 'Oh, Lynda *Hodgkiss* –
My, but initiative pays!
And they say there's no good in the young ones
Nowadays!'

Well, Lynda's birthday fell that week.
Mother, naturally, baked a cake
With nineteen candles like tiny deodorant sprays
Ablaze. The bell kept ringing:
Neighbour after neighbour
Stopping by the door. Soon enough they were singing
She's a jolly good fellow, so
Fresh, what's more.

Father and Mother, with a prizewinner under their roof
Those summer TV nights,
Felt chuckles were in order at
Three-pronged deodorant ads. Take MANTRAP,
The Freshener That Bites.

   First off: fragrance. ('Listening, Lynda?')
   Second off: dryness. ('Hear that, Lynda?')
   Third: prevention of clothing stains.

31

'TELL THAT TO LYNDA!' they'd yell
And laugh like drains.

Well, it couldn't last for ever, that was for sure.
But those were the days when the family was happy
And, thanks to Lynda, *everyone*
Felt secure.

Personal Advertisement

TASTY GEEZER/STUCK IN SNEEZER/YEAR BEFORE/GETS
   OUT/
SEEKS/SLOW-WITTED/GIANT-TITTED/SOCIOLOGIST
   VISITOR/
WHO LIKES/TO MESS ABOUT/

BLOKE NEEDS POKE/SEND PICS/BOX 6/

MASON/COUNCILLOR/MAGISTRATE/SOMETIME/CONSERVATIVE/
CANDIDATE/JOGGER/SQUASH-PLAYER/FIRST-CLASS SHAPE/
SEEKS SIMILAR/VIEW RAPE/

BLOKE NEEDS POKE/SEND PICS/BOX6/

SAD DOG/SEEKS TAIL/OLD BEAST/GROWN FRAIL/SNIFFING/
WORLD/FEELS MORE THAN/BITOUTOF/HELL WITH
   THAT/HUNTS/
OLDER CAT/TO MEET/GRAB/BEAT THE/SHITOUTOF/

BLOKE NEEDS POKE/SEND PICS/BOX 6/

WHAT/THE WINTER/NEEDS/IS STARLIGHT/WHAT/THE
   BLIND MAN/
NEEDS/IS LUCK/WHAT DIS BOY/NEED IS A/WEEK IN DE/SACK/
WID WUNNADEM/REAL/BIGASS SISTERS/DAT/COMES/LIKE A
   TRUCK/

BLOKE NEEDS POKE/SEND PICS/BOX 6/

LONG-FACED/LANKY/EVANGELICAL/WIFE
   EVANGELICAL/INTEREST/
SANKEY/MOTHER-IN-LAW/EVANGELICAL/CRANKY/SEEKS
   ANYBODY/
VIEW/HANKY-PANKY/

BLOKE NEEDS POKE/SEND PICS/BOX6/

PRIME MINISTER/FANCYING/CHANGE OF PACE/PLANS SPOT OF/
NONSENSE/BACK AT HER PLACE/ON REGULAR BASIS/NO AIRS/
GRACES/WOMEN OR MEN/POP IN/FOR A NAUGHTY/AT NO. TEN/

ONE PART/IRISH/THREE PARTS/PISSED/SIX FOOT/SEVEN AND/
NEVER BEEN/KISSED/WHERE/ARE YOU/

BLOKE NEEDS POKE/BOX6/
FORGET ABOUT THE PICS

One in One

Hall Hill dropped softly to the town
   I knew when I was small
And halfway up and halfway down
   Hall Hill there rose Hill Hall.
Hill Hall, I never dared to press,
   And can't now think I will,
The bell at your serene address,
   Simply: Hill Hall, Hall Hill.
And so the equilibrium
   I might have learnt is dead
And now all hell, Hill Hall, has come
   To stay, Hall Hill, instead.

Three Little Pigs to the Bar

In the *Unanointed*
Head where they'd defected,
Three, disappointed,
Sat: the Not Elected.
Time was more disjointed
Than they had expected.

One said Nothing.

Two, disaffected,
In the unappointed
Bar they'd not selected:
Neither one Anointed.
Time was more disjointed
Than they had expected.

One said Nothing.

One, unrequited,
In the not intended,
Casually ignited
World never mended.
Nothing would be righted
By the time it ended.

One said Nothing.

None, undefended,
In the dimmer-lighted,
Bitterly expended
Day to be benighted.
By the time it ended
Nothing would be righted.

None went home.

Question, Reply, Riposte

Exploded into our conversation
Like a diver surfacing with the bends
A wild-eyed man with a god-sized question,
Crying, 'The average dog, my friends,

He can sleep all day. We *work*. Then tell me,
Why does the dog die sooner, eh?'
'Their systems. Smaller.' 'Their what?' 'Systems.'
Said, 'Sod your system,' dived away.

Exits

1
The dead men will not abdicate the gardens.
They have unfinished business
With the light.

Rolled mist in dripping lime trees,
Lament of lawns, the raining
Day becoming night.

2
The great love that feeds us
Would feed us
To the wind.

3
Or,

As the little boy said who found
A dead one in a dustbin:

Somebody's thrown away
A perfectly good cat.

The Yoke

After the war, she was saying, he bought the house back
For nothing, practically nothing at all, but the house
Had come to be wilderness then and the spreading gardens
Desert or moonscape, cratered and churned as though
By tanks and bombs – like Africa, not Ayrshire.

> *She couldn't have told you when*
> *The marriage stopped in his face*
> *Where she wasn't anyone.*

Like Ayrshire, not like Africa, the cold
And the squalling rain. Raw-fingered, they set to,
Fitting the panelled rooms that bucked and creaked
On the wind like sailing ships in a storm and the children
Were screaming gulls that ravened on her heart.

> *She couldn't have told you when*
> *The marriage stopped in his face*
> *Where she wasn't anyone.*

All day they hacked at the land, dug, sawed, wheeled
   swaying
Barrows of corpse-wet, heavy-as-corpses earth
Down the wide droves of the garden, made violent sex
Most nights in his mother's bedroom:
Energy torn from exhaustion like despair.

> *She couldn't have told you when*
> *The marriage stopped in his face*
> *Where she wasn't anyone.*

In a broken outhouse, smelling of stone and blood,
He found the ploughshare perfectly, like stored
Furniture, draped in a sheet of white deadnettles
And sharp-edged hogweed. Soon the blade was honed
And the yoke of rope reefed on with its three hard loops.

> She couldn't have told you when
> The marriage stopped in his face
> Where she wasn't anyone.

So it came that friends from Edinburgh surprised them,
Her and the two boys, stumbling in tears and terror,
Hauling the great blade that he drove behind them
And then they looked up and she laughed, of course, he
   laughed,
A joke, to be found like this, of course it had been.

> And they saw in his empty face
> Quite clearly what he was
> And what she had become.

Iron City Love Song

Monongahela,
Allegheny,
Pittsburg civic
Fountain, flow

Down below
The Pittsburg Hilton,
Roll on in
To O-hi-o.

I am thinking
Of my darling,
Miles and miles
Away from me.

All I see,
Dark fork of rivers,
Now she goes
By E-ri-e.

Monongahela,
I am dreaming,
Allegheny,
Of the sea

Where the waters
Leap together.
In her arms
I soon shall be.

From Cheshire

for Anna

Come home safe: I think of you driving
  Over the Runcorn Bridge in our senile car,
Its toothless ratchets, arthritic pistons conniving
  To take me away from wherever you are,

Its steering like that old prostitute working a living
  On Huskisson Street outside our door:
Its raggedy brake shoes thin as the wind, giving
  Nothing but ice to your foot on the floor.

Please come home: I think of you leaving
  For ever, coming from Cheshire, only the snow
And the night and the endless black road, no retrieving
  Of you: without me, wherever I go.

Campionesque for Anna

When I lay down where I had lain with you
Some many nights, beloved, of the days
Lit by your sun, I dreamed all touch untrue,
Error my star and darkness all my ways
Till where I lay, I lay again with you.

Till where I go, I go again with you
Through all the days, beloved, and the nights
By your sweet self illumined, I can do
Not one good thing: not till your beauty lights
Me where I go, and go again with you.

Birthday Poem for Gavin Ewart

Guests of the hell-hot Plough Hotel
   In Cheltenham one mild
October midnight, at the bell
   We waited, shoes enisled
By little pecking waves of leaves;
   To Autumn reconciled

But *captivated* by the Night
   Porter. Tunes and rhymes
Must, we agreed, be set in flight
   To hymn the toils and times
Of one who in the book of life
   And looks WAS . . . Captain Grimes!

Antiquely modern, like New York,
   The DRINKS DISPENSER he
Loudly unleashed. To flatter talk,
   Our clanging coins set free
The mini-whiskies. Each contained
   A midget's heated pee

That tipped, a liquid After Eight
   To potent predecessors,
In toothmugs, warmed our Great Debate
   Of craft and its possessors,
Of live and lichened literature,
   Of poets and professors.

Of Walter de la Mare; likewise
   Of Walter de la Whitman,
Of boomers vasty as fen skies,
   Of jotters-down in Pitman,
Of Whitehouse leanings in the Second
   Charles' bum-and-tit man.

Of Craig and Kathleen Raine we spoke,
  Of phantom-struck or feely
Visionaries, of dreams that woke
  In mellow mouths or mealy,
Of Robert Louis Stevenson
  And Robert Louis Creeley.

Of weight, and air, and brevity,
  Of tears within the terse,
Of dark along the levity:
  The haywain by the hearse.
Of mournful, curious, scornful, spurious,
  Loved light-heavy verse.

Of Arthur Conan Doyle we sang
  And Arthur Conan Crooke,
The story-telling Georgian gang –
  Most, worth another look:
Of editors and predators
  Who make or break a book.

Of John Crowe Ransome, John Crowe Fuller,
  Singing late and soon,
Of Wilfreds Owen, Gibson, Wooller,
  Men that pack a tune
In mud to flight reality,
  Converted, through the moon.

Dear Gavin, Grimes was long in bed
  Or drowned. God send him joy . . .
(Each poet in his troubled head
  Is 'in the soup, old boy',
His little vision more than life
  His Dream, his Rest, his Toy).

Dear Gavin, Grimes was long in bed,
  Exhausted, or expired
And buying boys among the dead
  When you and I retired
From that inquiry natural warmth
  And midgets' piss had fired.

The little leaves go twirling round,
  Cracked make-up in their shards;
Windy and vain as Ezra Pound,
  The season strews its cards
But one says HAPPY BIRTHDAY to
  The best of men and bards!

I wish you joy and long delight
  In heart and flowing pen!
I wish, as on that hell-hot night
  To tope with you — as then,
To talk of verse and 'laughter-smithing'
  Many times again!

It's not quite what I meant to say;
  It changes once you start.
Accept upon your natal day
  This rather-less-than-art,
Imperfect fiction from the head —
  Affection from the heart.

I Found South African Breweries Most Hospitable

Meat smell of blood in locked rooms I cannot smell it,
Screams of the brave in torture loges I never heard nor
  heard of
Apartheid I wouldn't know how to spell it,
None of these things am I paid to believe a word of
For I am a stranger to cant and contumely.
I am a professional cricketer.
My only consideration is my family.

I get my head down nothing to me or mine
Blood is geysering now from ear, from mouth, from eye,
How they take a fresh guard after breaking the spine,
I must play wherever I like or die
So spare me your news your views spare me your homily.
I am a professional cricketer.
My only consideration is my family.

Electrodes wired to their brains they should have had
  helmets,
Balls wired up they should have been wearing a box,
The danger was the game would turn into a stalemate,
Skin of their feet burnt off I like thick woollen socks
With buckskin boots that accommodate them roomily
For I am a professional cricketer.
My only consideration is my family.

They keep falling out of the window they must be clumsy
And unprofessional not that anyone told me,
Spare me your wittering spare me your whimsy,
Sixty thousand pounds is what they sold me
And I have no brain. I am an anomaly.
I am a professional cricketer.
My only consideration is my family.

Sweet Blue

These children of light, to the tune light began,
Danced in out of Chaos, played catch-as-catch-can
With happiness, live in the road where they ran:

Sweet Blue, kind Ronald and John the Fat Man.

Then one of the heartburst and two of the crab,
Each came to lie cold as a fish on a slab,
And each went away in a shiny black cab:

Sweet Blue, kind Ronald and John the Fat Man.

Blue played the piano and Blue, she could sing,
Of all jolly fat men fat John was the king,
I scarcely think Ronald did one cruel thing:

Sweet Blue, kind Ronald and John the Fat Man.

But everything worked out according to plan.
To each of the angels his space and his span.
And I shall continue to grieve, as I can,

Sweet Blue, kind Ronald and John the Fat Man.

Underneath the Archers
or
What's all this about Walter's Willy?

Everyone's on about Walter's willy
   Down at the Bull tonight.
He's done Dan's sheep and he's done them silly –
He's had young Phil and his daughter's filly –
   And folk don't think it's right.

   Folk know it can't be right.

No, the chat's not prim and the chat's not proper,
   Down at the Bull tonight,
'Cos everyone's on about Walter's whopper
And telling tales of his terrible chopper –
   And folk don't think it's right.

Sid Perks has drained the bitter cup
   Down at the Bull tonight.
Can't stand . . . or sit . . . or speak . . . or sup . . .
Walter got him while bottling up –
   And folk don't think it's right.

   Folk know it can't be right.

He got poor Polly while drawing a cork
   Down at the Bull tonight.
And Doris is still too ill to talk –
And Mrs Perkins can hardly walk –
   And folk don't think it's right.

There's in-depth discussion of every facet,
   Down at the Bull tonight,
Of Walter's gigantic natural asset –
Carries as far as Penny Hasset –
   (Folk know that can't be right)

   Folk know it can't be right.

Poor old Dan's a broken man
   Down at the Bull tonight.
Got locked in the back of Walter's van
With its ghastly height, unearthly span —
   And folk don't thing it's right.

Found him alone in the woods on Sunday
   (Down at the Bull tonight),
Had him all day and most of Monday —
That was the end of poor Joe Grundy —
   Folk don't think it's right.

   Folk *know* it can't be right.

It wasn't a Gainsborough nor an El Greco
   (Down at the Bull tonight)
Brought dozens of coach-loads out for a dekko —
But a photo-fit in the *Borchester Echo* —
   Folk don't think it's right.

Nobody understands it fully,
   Down at the Bull tonight,
The monstrous *range* of it. Was it by pulley
It scaled Grey Gables and whopped Jack Woolley?
   Folk don't think it's right.

   Folk *know* it can't be right.

There's coaches come from Ware and Wigan,
   Down at the Bull tonight,
From Wales and Wallasey, out for a swig an'
A sizing-up of Walter's big 'un —
   And folk don't think it's right.

Yes, everyone's on about Walter's thuggery,
   Down at the Bull tonight,
His *cattle*-courting, his *sheep* skullduggery,
Piggery jiggery-pokery buggery —
   Folk don't think it's right.

   Folk *know* it can't be right.

Even the Vicar's been muttering, 'F*** it,'
  Down at the Bull tonight,
'There's nowhere left he hasn't stuck it –
I *wish* old Walter would kick the bucket –
  He knows it can't be right!'

Folk know it CAN'T BE RIGHT!

Agony Calories

The cooling seaward echo of his screams
Locked in the flesh:

Succulent beyond dream, a live-boiled lobster,
Terror-fresh!

How much pain can you eat?

But wait —
Given a choice in the matter,
Our friend Mr Lobster
Would very much rather
You didn't plunge him *straight*
Into a pan of boiling seawater
(You knew that by the noise)
But *simmered* him to a *gradual* death
At eighty-five degrees, a method
Mr Lobster *very much enjoys!*

(You can tell by the way he
Bobs about:
Stick a weight on the lid so
He can't pop out!)

Now. See how much —
But wait!

On page two hundred and seventy-eight
Of *Fish Cookery* by Jane Grigson —
'How To Cut Up Live Lobster'
So the lobster doesn't cut up! He'll love it.
No fooling with boiling and cooling. Just
Winkle out the place
Where the tail joins up with the carapace
And whack it with a cleaver. Smash him in half!

You'll get a thrill –
And you'll hear Mr Lobster laughing,
You'll hear Mr Lobster laughing,
Yes, you'll hear Mr Lobster laughing
All the way to the grille!

Cut off the claws and crack them.
Crosscut the tail into slices.
Stack them.
Likewise, *lengthwise*
Split the head: then
Mr Lobster
Must be dead! It's

Alla marinara,
A l'americaine,
Courchamps,
Bonnefoy,
A
La
Crème.

A la mayonnaise . . .
A la Charentaise . . .

Newburg!
    A l'aurore!
A l'anise!
    THERMIDOR!

Consume the entire insides of the arthropod
Except for the black
Intestinal canal and the sac
Of grit. Savour

Every bit. Then
                leaning well back
In your rockpool,
                letting
The slurrying sucked salt and the
                        plankton pick
Your mandibles clean,
                between

The pincers of your
                bigger but niftier
      LEFT
        CLAW

Nip off the tip of a huge cigar!
Ignite delight in the gloom
Of your basement home: a treat to tell
Time by the barnacles
Squeezing your shell
As over the flame you wait for the pungent
Pain to bunch and mass:
It's a natural state: it's only

Natural Mr Lobster
And natural gas.

The Power of Prayer

Very, very little of his garden
  Did God elect to seed.
The rest he leased to utter, outer blankness,
  Invaded by the rankness
    Of not a single weed.

Many, many mansions has his dwelling.
  His own bedsit is small.
A vast and speechless city crumbles round it.
  Never a one has found it
    Anywhere at all.

The Day Room

(from Kendal Ward, Rainhill Mental Hospital)

1

Many are non-plussed
By the unexpected behaviour of their clothes
And have mislaid forever
The art of wearing the face.

Gums wedged tight or mouths
Locked open in a scream that travels inward
Homelessly:

Here we all are on your holy mountain.

It's a little bit nippy up here on the mountain
For some are shivering, never
Stop shivering, also

Unseasonably warm. That man
Is caked with lava, head to hip.

2

Come in, come in,
Don't shut the door.
Take care your feet
Don't touch the floor.

Come on, come on.
Avoid the wall.
Whatever you do
Don't breathe at all.

Stand back, stand back.
What is it? Ask
But whisper through
Your cotton mask.

Back out. Make sure
The door is closed.
Now wash your hands
And burn your clothes.

3
Joan's mouth is a crematorium.
Six years after her husband died
It burns and bleeds and weeps, she cannot beat
His flaring ashes down with her tongue.

All in the mind, and pain
(What was said? What left unsaid?)
A child of the mind
That eats the mother.

The widow is burned alive.

4
Where cigarettes are the entire economy
Domestic policy is locker-love.
Pink stones to arm the military,
White coats for the judiciary,
One hall in hell for all of the above.

5
The male nurses, without exception,
Corpulent, good-natured,
Moustachioed forty-year-olds.
Five of them. How can this be?

They must have a club where they stand and swap
Rounds and jokes and mistakes and moustaches,
Taking each other's paunches
Like a pulse.

6
Our road's a green carbolic corridor
Off which on certain days the sun
Ripens in small groves. In one

I found her crying because she had lost her lipstick
And, so she said, her bones.

The sun poured down.

We found the lipstick, couldn't find the bones.

7
Unspeakable blue
Observed
Through unbreakable glass.

How long have those humanoid beech-limbs,
Their green-dust glaze a parody of spring,
Aped inmates? Patients here
Slept on hay and this afternoon
We queue like sheepish children
For the tablet trolley,
Candy counter that won't divert
The all-day double-honking donkey bray
Of Josie,
Without mind. Or is it
Meaning, is it
What we call gladness in the natural world
As the faint cry of those gulls
Dancing over the kitchen pickings:

A wheeling above
The leavings, mirth
In what she might have been?

8
Pat threw herself away
From babies, from
A seventh floor. Foetus-coiled
She sleeps all day
On two sun-coloured plastic chairs,
Snug by the mother-warmth
Of the radiator.

9
Reg was a Ship's Officer,
Blue Funnel, Ellermans.

Alert on the bridge and likewise
Scholarly in the chartroom,

He wheeled great cargoes
Through the Southern seas.

Struck off the pool, he slumps
Blindly on the windowsill,

His head plunged into his arms
That are guiding nothing.

10
One sits fluttering, fluttering.
Poor, pale moth stuck through with a pin.

One seeks me out to whisper
Extraordinary confidences
Concerning the holy ghost
And a computer. One

Rages up and down the day room
Shouting, 'It's shite.' Everyone's right.

11
The evening canteen
Is where like minds meet.
Eruptions of senile fisticuffs,
Dancing and even
Love I've seen:

One childishly sprawled
On another's knee,
Sucked kisses with cigarettes
Endangering the endearments.

Behind a partition,
The healthful sane are playing badminton.
The shuttlecock soars to heaven like a searchlight,
Drifts to the earth like snow.

Our side
Has a stout Edwardian billiard table,
Permanently sheeted,
Reserved for the diversions of the dead.

12

Many streets in the hospital,
'The largest of any kind
In Europe' when it was built and many
Minds within the mind.

'The shifting population
Of a grid-iron city.'
Pathetic co-operations and courtesies,
Hunger and pity.

This is your holy mountain,
Your shallow grave.
When nothing's left this is what's left
To save.